Love Without Distance

A HEARTSCAPE OF ART AND VERSE

DOROTHY BURY SHAW

This book is dedicated with love to those brave and beautiful seekers I continue to meet along the streets and byways of this journey without distance.

A message to my readers,

I fell in love with a divine Presence as a very small girl, before I knew there was a word for it - God. My constant Companion was a loving, supportive, formless, ever-present source of joy. The existence of this benevolent Being was undeniable. But as I grew and absorbed the teachings of my elders, the purity of my early perception was replaced with a grander view, full of ancient stories, rules to follow, doctrines to accept, and responsibilities to keep. As everything began to shift into new form, a distance seemed to grow between me and the one who was my All in All. Thus, a lifetime of longing began for the return of the exquisitely uncomplicated relationship I had once shared with my Beloved.

Through more than three decades of exploration, within the reaches of many welcoming branches of Christianity, through study of beautiful eastern religions and the refreshing fellowship of universalists in varied traditions, and through joyful immersion in *A Course in Miracles*, I began to experience again a greater Whole, and the depth of that all-encompassing closeness I knew as a child, a Oneness, a profound Interbeing, a *Love Without Distance*.

My art and poetry reflect this pathway and through it, I am at last nearly where I first began with my Divine. Somewhere along the line, I returned to my church community, drawing from the fellowship, ancient ritual, modern music, a rich mystic tradition and a sense of stewardship for the earth and its many cultures. I'll never be bound to one teaching in the traditional sense, but it no longer matters. I am already Home.

Please enjoy *Love Without Distance*, from my heart to yours.

Dorothy Berry Shea

ACKNOWLEDGEMENTS

To Stephen Shaw, my dear husband, with love and thanksgiving for your kindness, patience and forgiving spirit, never judging or criticizing. You have provided me with the comfort and safety needed to explore the uncharted waters of my life.

To Monica Shaw and Stephanie Shaw, my precious daughters, you have constantly inspired me with your independence and courage. You each have forged your own path in life and I am awed watching your lives unfold. I do so cherish our times together … the laughter, the mischief and sweetly secret understandings we share.

To Helen Bury, my beloved mother now in heaven, you taught me about God at a very young age, and lived your life with a beautiful, simple, uncomplicated faith. As a teacher, you filled our home with books. Through you I found a lifelong hunger for learning and a love for reading. Now I relish a deep and intimate spirituality, learning from your example that this inner reality is the one that matters most in living an abundant life.

To Bruno Bury, my incredible father, now age 97, you have always encouraged me to be a writer. As a young girl you once told me, "Still waters run deep." And I have spent all these years marveling that you saw something in me beyond what I could see. I continue to explore what lies beneath those still waters. Your sensitive heart, your pluck and drive, your tender sentiment and tenacity – these qualities continue to inspire.

To my darling siblings, Kathy Lewandowski, Robert Bury, Sue Otero and Sandra Bury, you keep me humble, support me in my dreams and fill my heart in ways too many to count. My love for you touches the stars.

To Jordan Luff, my little grandchild. With you I am a child again, connecting to your innocence, pure love and joy. With you I am experiencing nature anew, at your eye level, the smallest details and the biggest moments. With you I am face to face and heart to heart with Love itself.

To Jill Sorensen Kopin, treasured friend and helper, you offered to assist when I was struggling with the overwhelming task of presenting and showing my art. You can never know how much it has meant to me to have your support, kindness, big heart and beautiful soul along this journey.

To Don Ozimek, my dear, longtime friend and fellow artist, you were the first to speak of truths I had never experienced before. They all deserved to be known. You were a portal into a world more real than this material facade. And through you, in 1991, I found A Course in Miracles which continues to be my guide.

To Katheryne Clippert, for many, many hours of extraordinary, life-changing conversation shared over the course of several truly incredible years. You fed my fire and supported my calling to pursue art and poetry, even as the swan song began to play and our time together gracefully reached its summit.

To Kenny Swisher, my dearest of friends during a time of life when my heart was healing and wakening to a purpose grander than any I could have imagined. Your words and beautiful spirit have stayed with me and motivated me to write.

To my powerful sisterhood of cherished friends, amazing women of talent, strength, intellect, spirit, wisdom and beauty, you each are a precious gift. I delight in all we continue to share, for it feeds my soul like nothing else could. You inspire me and bring me close enough to dance with my highest self.

ART CATALOG

POEMS

HOUSE FOR GOD

I will build a house for God within my painting,

a home for the universe in each line,

a pillow for consciousness in each color.

God's lips are my ink,

laying a divine kiss upon the wound

humanity won't allow to heal.

CASTER OF SHADOWS

Our shadows exist because there first was Light.

BLESSED IS SHE

BLESSED IS SHE

Her purpose was ordained
when the sun first lit the sky.

All of creation moved softly, age to age,
with the most exquisite patience
preparing a place just for her.

And this very night as she sleeps,
the mighty Voice speaks
and a hush falls upon the land.

The universe listens and responds
with the hum of timeless vibrations.

Forever will it seek
to deliver her to her destiny.

For blessed is she.
And a blessing, given to one,
is evermore a blessing for all of creation.

EVERYDAY PRIESTESS

Everyday Priestess

She met Him

in the space between two horizons

and called out,

"Here I am."

He answered,

"Here we are, for I am with you."

From that day forward she found her joy

in loving those He entrusted to her.

For she did it on behalf of the One who sent her.

All cultures, all creeds, all colors, all ages … they came.

Upon each suffering face she saw His and responded with Love.

Buried deep within their swollen eyes she felt Him,

and bathed them with Love.

Sweet Love. Perfect Love. Always Love.

For in the space between two horizons

there was nothing but … Love.

HALLELUJAH QUARTET

Hallelujah Quartet

A woman, a songbird

and the morning sun

burst into song.

Voices held high,

a perfect union

of sound, color and light.

They sing

of adoration to the One they love

above all others.

Suspended in time,

it is a song without end.

You are wondering,

who is the fourth member of this quartet?

Dear one, it is you.

For you have joined in the spirit of their song.

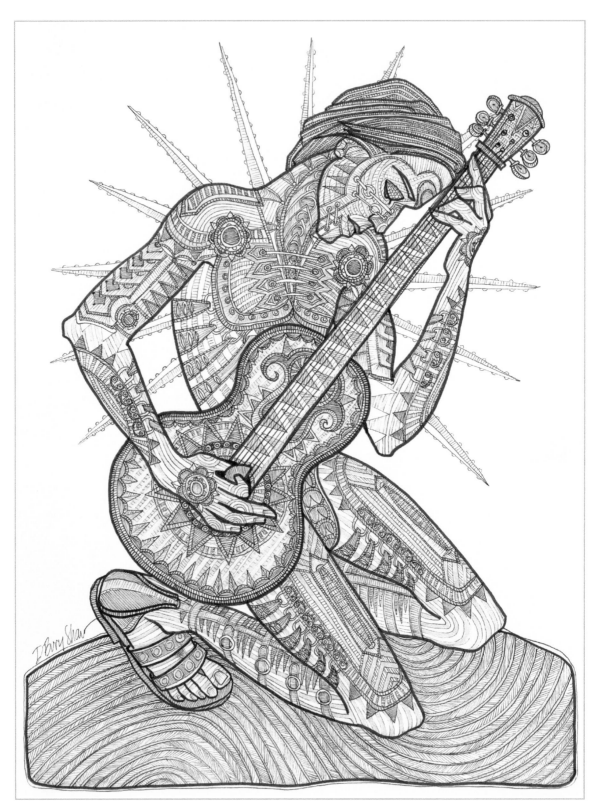

CANTICLE OF THANKSGIVING

BRAVE

Branches tease the heavens,
and below the frost line
roots are frayed, loosely-knitted
strands of yesterday.

Within this forgotten grove
his sighs gather like soldiers,
forming row upon row.

Vigilant votive candles,
brave, so brave,
dodging breezes,
burning strong.

BAPTISM

And so, I laid my broken parts
where the sycamore fell down.
They shall become my stepping stones.
I know not where I'm bound.

It won't matter where they lead me
or when at last I'm there,
with willow bark and lavender,
tucked in my braided hair.

And if I ever trace my steps
right back to where I started,
I'll find a songbird's garden there,
and the font where gates had parted.

REAL

Seemingly separate,

distinct from each other,

opposing planes, shifting and falling,

static in motion.

What is real?

A collision of truths,

a clash of opinions,

conflicting perspectives,

forceful forward, holding back.

What is real?

The sacred calm, the secular call,

the cutting betrayal, the forgiving flame,

patterns in flux,

together alone, connected apart.

What is real?

Staring into the golden mirror, I see you.

Looking at you, I see myself.

Your wounds are my wounds.

Our stories drift away, the slate is smooth.

This is real.

HER HEART, HIS ONLY HOME

Her Heart, His Only Home

A man of simple needs and few words,

he held no malice in his heart.

The hidden nook he built for himself in the clock tower

was stacked with books which left no room for dreams or dragons.

Absorbed in his world of peculiar maps and foreign script,

he asked for little in life,

except for permission to love her.

Now… she was born to wander

and came to him from a place vast as the sky.

She thrived in traversing a wilderness

that stretched across time and space.

Her heart, carried safely within her, was a sacred place.

And thus, she chose carefully who would enter this sanctum.

But in his carefully ordered routine she found solace.

So, she welcomed him into her heart,

providing a space that was his alone.

She silently promised him the very things he'd already given her.

She'd tread softly and ask no questions.

She knew her velvet heart was his only home.

READY FOR DAWN

I Am Ready

I am all set to begin,

I am ready to let go,

I am primed to explore,

I am girded now to know.

I am opening my heart,

I am willing now to see.

I am able to forgive,

I am content to simply be.

I am reaching for the Light,

I am reaching deep inside,

I am unplugging all that was,

I am welcoming the tide.

I am washed of all my errors.

I am cleansed of all mistakes.

I am borne on a surging arc.

I am.

PEACEFUL WALK OF TRUST

Let Me Remind You

He scattered her illusions across a milky field of stars.
Then with utmost care, He etched lines through each orbit,
whole notes, quarters, triplets and chords,
a composition for His orchestra.

Together they sat and listened
to the perfect lullaby of rise and fall,
the majestic swell which followed the pounding hush.
Then gently He sang to her.

My very own child,
do not allow those who hurt you
to teach you who you are.

Let me remind you …

My darling,
I modeled every faction of your being.
I know you deeply where no man can see.
With mercy, I visit every pocket of your fears,
And I mend the unlatched portal
where your sword flashes
golden sparks against the night.

Let me remind you …

I formed every fold of your lovely cortex.
Oh breathe, my tender traveler, breathe.
I relish the sublime swell of every intake.
The rising sun shall infuse every fiber of your being,
I press my seal upon your beating heart.

Little one, you have tried too long.
Rest, be the space between my notes.
Push aside the veil of wishes that falls across your face,
for it casts a shadow upon my perfect creation.

A PRAYER'S RELEASE

A Prayer's Release

Gone... the thief's hungry reach for her dreams.

Silenced... the inner voices that deceived her.

Banished... the fear that followed each mistake.

Uncovered... the freedom to choose a better way.

Returned... the peace of Love's embrace.

Discovered... the merge into Oneness.

SIMPLE PLEASURES

Undoing

An ordinary day,

with extraordinary circumstance.

Others closed their eyes as she opened hers.

Then she remembered ...

to see without judgement.

Several deep breaths later

with tears in her eyes, she saw anew.

So, she lifted her chin.

She summoned the Light,

She placed the wholeness of her being

in God's embrace.

Eyes still open, still breathing,

she gathered the four winds of change within her.

Rolling, pounding, racing, bursting

they came.

Swirling, tumbling, rustling, weaving

they came.

From a roar to a whisper

they came.

Her stillness was their undoing.

And she said,

I accept.

IN YOUR EYES

My reflection glows in your eyes.

Still I cannot see your face.

I am small and You are endless.

I am trust and You are grace.

I long to breathe You, live to know You,

your clear waters are my balm.

And I will walk a thousand miles

to trace the lines that cross your palm.

I will claim this golden moment.

Nothing else exists in time.

As we join we lose our edges,

perfect Oneness, so sublime.

Darling Traveler

Find me …

In the breeze that carries seeds of summer wildflowers.
Their colors shall stretch for miles just for you.

In the shallow stream that rushes to wash your road-weary feet.
Pause, darling traveler, and be cleansed.

In the tree tops where each leaf holds one of your secrets to my Light.
I gather them all to create your new beginnings.

Find me …

Above the pines rimmed in moonlight where a golden star winks just for you.
It tells you I am near.

In the magnolia bud's promise that it will open in my time.
It cannot be rushed, but dearest, the bloom will come.

In the warmth of the rock where the speckled lizard rests.
I have created a place for you, too, and will walk with you there.

Find me …

In the crane's call as it passes overhead.
He knows his southbound path and you were born to know yours.

In the markings that cover the sleeping doe
As I have protected her, my little one, I am also protecting you.

In the embrace of another, where hearts kiss and beats synchronize in song.
I am Love and you were fashioned in my image.

POISED FOR FLIGHT

Poised for Flight

She braces herself
and turns to face the wind,
about to take a great leap.

Part warrior, part huntress, part angel,
she is prepared for what may come.

Soft of heart,
with a might greater than her own,
she sees past the danger
and beyond those
who cannot yet understand.

Nothing can break
who she was born to be.

FROM WOMB TO HEART

From Womb to Heart

It began long before her child was born…

the deep sense of knowing.

The spark of life within her

held divine purpose.

Her tender womb would serve

as the infant's first cradle.

The little one would be lulled to sleep

hearing the soothing beat

of the heart that would join with God

in loving her for all time.

THE MERMAID'S SECRET

The Mermaid's Secret

The sea was angry that day.

Strong and fearless, she was not amused.

In an instant she would disappear

into those flashing waters…

down, down…

perhaps to skim the ocean floor

where the pirate ship rested,

its trove known to her alone.

On second thought,

today she will swim the endless tunnels

of her Lover's veins.

In the end it's all the same.

With every treasure

she found a certain calm

the deeper she did go.

MIGHTY ROOTS

MIGHTY ROOTS

Close as we could ever be
to All that was and All yet to be,
In hallowed depths that no one sees
I touch you and you touch me.

In loamy pith and glacial clay
our stories form, we find our way.
Oh, it is Love that holds us tight.
We're standing strong, washed in Light.

STAR OF PEACE

Untamed Stillness

Come into the silent presence of

carousing clouds,

wandering streams,

bursting blooms,

nesting geese,

dancing sunbeams,

waving marsh grasses,

hovering bees.

Feral stillness combs through

the tangled strands that bind me.

Undaunted, it infuses

my awakening stretch,

my soul's reach,

my spirit soaring,

vibrations stirring,

bold inner space

where life is exuberant!

Come into the presence of

living, breathing, drumming, humming,

stillness.

Come be with the One

whose essence is Light.

THE RAINDANCE

She stepped into the downpour to be cleansed.
But gently He corrected her intention.

"No, my child."

She sighed.

"I sent the rain that you might dance.
I have seen how you love to twirl in puddles."

Oh, how He loved her.

She replied, her head lowered.

"But I am soiled. A mess."

Her travels had taken her down some unlit, shabby alleys
and along a few mucky backroads.

He took her hand, extended his arm
and she twirled around playfully.
He delighted in her joyous abandon.

"Where did the stains go?" He asked her.

"I cannot find them!" she exclaimed.

"Little girl, they never existed."

GRIEF

Certain as a crescent moon
a fissure opens in the heavens.
Time has come.
He must go to her again.

Tugged into black undercurrents
she wisely surrenders for she will not drown here.
Oh, that these waters might cleanse her
mingle with her tears, carrying her
buoyant to another bend of the cone-shaped spiral.

With the patience of a thousand kisses
her Ambassador lifts her back to her feet
and ushers her around one more curve.

This cannot be rushed.

From throat, to temple, to eyelid, to ear
the touch of his lips follows each beat of her breaking heart.

It is an endless journey.
And her faithful Escort knows
she must walk every step of it.

Grief, your sweetness runs deep
for you are but Love's other face when soul meets soul.

The parting can seem so real.

And so the great Ambassador
leads her gently onward.

They enter a covered bridge,
dark and precarious.
They tread from death to life, from past to present,
from future to present, from distance to joining.

And the impossible happens.
She emerges once again
re-birthed, re-connected.

They will repeat their requiem march,
ring after ring
until day and night are no more.

GEMSTONES

GEMSTONES

Dear ones, loved ones
near and far, long gone and newly born
of the ancients and from unknown tribes,
carried to me on prevailing winds,
or fished from distant seas,
it only matters that we met.

Dear ones, loved ones
fallen from the summer skies, mined from black caverns,
marked by the searing tip of a branding iron,
or soothed by the cool waters along the river bed,
it only matters that we met,

Dear ones, loved ones,
colliding with unseen forces and sustaining injury
whether in the meeting or in the parting of our two souls,
it only matters that we met,

Dear ones, loved ones,
as misaligned surfaces of two magnets connecting in defiance of physics,
with a bond that escapes human understanding,
it only matters that we met.

Dear ones, loved ones,
as lyrical murmurations above the wheat fields
having whirled, drifted and crested as dark clouds
only to be dispersed as black, tattered lace stretched east to west,
it only matters that we met.

We were meant to be.

Now you have your own rightful place as a single, magnificent stone
among these strands that cross my heart.

You are always with me.
At any moment I can touch you, hold you
and feel the timeless presence of us again, and be stronger for it.

At some point in the crossing of our paths,
I must have paused long enough to see only your truest self,
your perfect innocence ... and nothing else.
In that sacred instant, coal became diamond,
joining you to me for all time.
It only matters that we met.

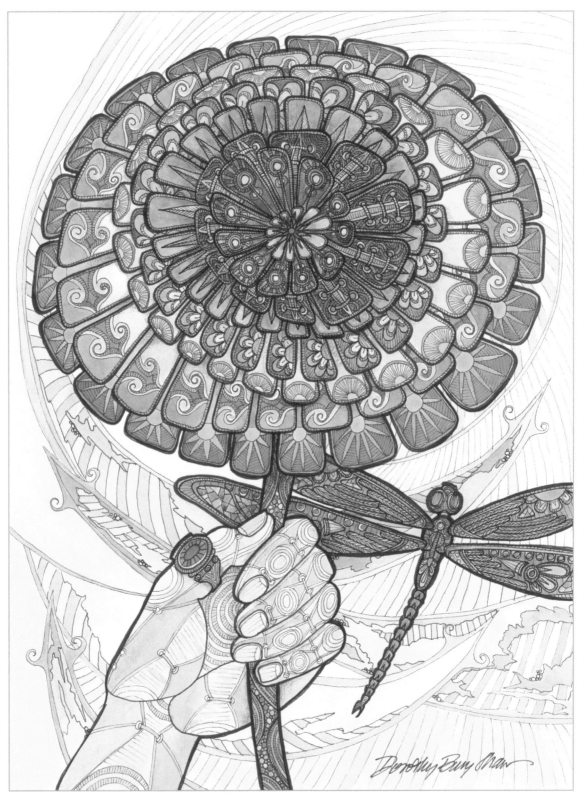

THE DRAGONFLY'S REFRAIN

THE DRAGONFLY'S REFRAIN

She had traveled many miles with many more to go.
Wearily, she paused to rest.
A dragonfly with prism wings landed on her wrist.
She smiled at her old friend.

"Yes, it's time." She told him.

She opened her pouch to lighten her load.
It contained treasures and trinkets, collected over time.
So small they were, but together they had become difficult to carry.
One by one she held each item to the sunlight.

Here was the lack of closure she'd tucked away,
and there laid a jury of mistakes and a tangle of mixed messages.
She found letters unsent and differences unresolved.
Added to these were the promises broken,
several strings of lies and
one deaf ear.

The dragonfly,
with an effortless lightness of being rose into the sky
where his eyes glittered like sapphires as he said...

"That was then, this is now."

She had held on mightily,
with her form bent and limbs aching
as if to abandon her cache would be stripping flesh from bone.

The worthless bundle, now seen in the light of day,
was stitched with dark tendrils of smoke and had started to smolder.
In one brilliant flash it all turned to ash,
only to be scattered by the flickering flurry of beating wings.

As she packed for the next leg of her journey,
her companion began to sing.

"Oh gather ye Love of every kind,
weightless, strong and stable.
With thankful heart suffused with grace,
thou art freed and wholly able."

In a twinkling the dragonfly was gone.
She continued on, leaving no bootprints.

LITTLE GROVE

THE LITTLE GROVE

From the delicate swirl

and hungry rumble

of Creation's own womb,

six tall trees arose.

With long arms they reached upward

to what remained unseen.

Their thirsty roots anchored downward

to drink deeply

of Love's gift-giving garden.

Six tall trees,

Still growing.

I do believe they've

touched the stars.

WORTHY OF TRUST

It Doesn't Go Away

It softens,

it deepens,

it steps back,

it moves closer,

but it doesn't go away.

It widens,

it narrows,

it climbs,

it falls,

it whispers,

it pleads,

it laughs,

it cries.

It hushes in the morning,

it whispers in the night.

It feeds me,

it starves me.

It's the skin around my heart,

and it doesn't go away.

WISER, STRONGER, BRAVER

Wiser, Stronger, Braver

With love she learned …

Reaching is touching.

Letting go is letting in.

Opening wide is holding close.

Thinking is choosing.

Through love she found …

Wisdom expanded intellect.

Strength replaced weakness.

Bravery overcame fear.

The flight of Love knows no bounds.

.

MASTERPIECE

In his compassion
he buried my dead.

Believing she knew best
she gave birth to my dreams.

They did not understand
this was my work to do.

O my dear ones,
comfort me in my grief.
Listen as my dreams shift into shape,
but do not spare me the pain I must bear.
Just be with me and hold me in your heart.

For I have learned,
through every break in the tower of my expectations
I breathe fresh, cleansing air.

Through the splitting boards of my weathered boat
I sip the purest waters of life.

Divine perfection,
with its many cracks and holes,
will always clear my frothy, high-minded clutter
and distill my saltiest tears.

The Master knows
as He loads his brush with paint
that what began as darkness will become shimmering light
in the most surprising ways.

Nameless

She, who would remain nameless,
only scattered diamonds
across the riverbed where he walked
and gave song to the chickadees outside his window.

She tuned the strings of his heart to the key of Be.

She put the blush in the roses where he stood before tomb stones
and filed away the thorns on the vine that climbed his walls.

She stitched them both to the moonlight
as it welcomed the dawn
then watched him break away in a freefall back into a black sky.

She lit a fire in his bones when the marrow ran dry
and wrapped a woolen blanket around his wounded heart.

She carried his darkest secrets to the pyre of nevermore
and pinned his tears to the clothesline
where the light turned them all to pearls.

In the end he wasn't hers to tend,
so she gathered all the diamonds and pearls,
and put them in the perfect pocket with a hole in it.

One by one they fell where needed most.
And like seeds, great things sprang forth,
new life where they landed.

LOTUS IN THE SUN

LOTUS IN THE SUN

The little seed lamented …
"You planted me in somber waters
where life had shed its skin
amidst the forsaken and unseen.
Then you called to me."

O come, little one!
Come into my Presence,
and the glory that awaits you.

She listened with wonder.
Impossible, undeniable, undeserved … yet true.

Was there a quiver along the edges of her being?
What held her to this flame she could not see?
Was there a kiss upon the tangled graveyard around her?
Had this tomb become her cradle
and Divine, the Hand that rocked it?

"Yes!" she cried.
"Here I come, O Light Divine …
to you, of you … yours."

Upon her acceptance came a resplendent rising,
while she was held in stillness,
through no power of her own,
a burgeoning luminescence,
a ripening chroma painted in light.

What Universe was this to greet her with song?
And then it paused …
She opened wide and strong, breathing the Light,
though standing still in darkness.

ONE GOLDEN INSTANT

One Golden Instant

Eyes lift to seek the sun.

Thoughts pause in the budding treetops

between droplets of rain.

Clinging... still clinging ...

to branches that bravely bore the long winter.

Little droplets... tiny fingers ... they cling.

I cling.

Oh, I cling.

Again, I have forgotten

the golden Light

patiently bleaching holes in grey clouds,

coaxing the sapling's first leaf to uncurl,

and silently returning

for me each day.

THIS TIME, THAT PLACE

THIS TIME, THAT PLACE

Standing here, everything seems different.

Looking 'round, nothing's really changed.

Can it be between one breath and another

an entire world's been rearranged?

Things came apart, with nothing left to hold them.

Yet here they are, falling into place.

What happened then hardly seems to matter.

No blame, or shame, it all has been erased.

I recall the walls we built between us.

The rocks were yours and the mortar was mine.

Nothing's left but a patch of scattered rubble

and the fragrance of lavender and pine.

So long ago, my prayers were filled with questions.

Year after year, no answers came my way.

Now I see I was asking the wrong questions.

My unspoken prayer was answered here today.

TENDER MERCIES

TENDER MERCIES

She called his name and Mercy answered.
It took a while,
but what is time but a learning curve
on life's winding journey?

It never mattered who was at fault,
what was spoken, or what was done.

Both were wrong, and both were right.

One day he left his ego hanging
like an icicle in the sunshine,
and she forgot to care about the outcome.

And so, they rested.
Beyond the battle ground, another world awaited them.

He would ask nothing of her there,
and with awe and reverence,
witness how her loving heart blossomed
and her radiance burned the shadows dry.

She would release her need of him,
and discover him anew as a helpmate and fellow pilgrim,
as the wildflower where her deepest appreciation flourished.

With his eyes, he traced forgiveness on her lips.
With each pulse of her heart
she drummed the song of her return.

THE RIVER'S EDGE

We, short of breath and long in years,
watch this fallen branch as it drifts upon the water.
It moves without effort.
We step softly onto it, light as a sparrow's song
as the shimmering current carries us onward.

Hand in hand, we settle
into the rhythm of the ripples
watching the blue heron hunting at the shoreline
as our heartaches come into view.
Our heads slowly turn as we follow each fractured dream
as it disappears behind the curve of woodlands.
And the heron takes flight.

Moving forward,
we pause to look with kindest moist eyes at each other,
I see my very self in you.

But soon a team of silver, quivering shadows
meets us around the river's bend.
Each one is chained to the next.
We know not what to do.
We cannot take them into our arms,
even as they plead,
even when the urge to do so gnaws at our heels,
for we would be pulled into the depths below.
The waters we travel are the tears they cry.
The figures grow distant, thin and pale as we pass them by.

Now the sun is setting,
and I have seen your other self.
And you have seen mine.
Our dark silhouettes stretch long enough,
to reach all the way back to where we began.
For though we journeyed many miles,
upon our crooked, twiggy raft
we now realize we never left the shore.

But a light glows in your soft eyes
as never before.
We are still hand in hand.
At long last, we have met for the first time.

WE COME AS ONE

WE COME AS ONE

Somewhere, between day and night,

as the fledgling tucks her beak beneath ruffled wings …

Someplace, between yesterday and tomorrow,

as the gold-dusted honey bee returns to the hive …

Somehow, between certainty and doubt,

as the fawn waits out the field storm in peace and stillness …

Someway, between joy and sorrow,

as the baby is born and a refugee breathes his last an ocean away …

We find our way.

Something sacred, something holy

arrives without a word

the instant we turn a corner,

settling upon the deepest shadows,

alighting softly,

like the hand of grace upon a quivering heart.

We come as one.

We are one footstep

crossing the threshold that brings us Home.

PERSEPHONE'S DAUGHTER

Persephone's Daughter

She fears not these dark days,
nor the molecular marvels of her underworld.
Real as they might appear, they hold no place
in the wakening spectrum of her consciousness.

With a fearless wisdom
and an emboldened knowing,
she does not blink at a discomforting awareness.

Around her, in the depths of blackness,
the earth's own alchemy molders with perfection.
What masquerades as dull, leaden silence
is weightless in this sanctum.
Root tips are etching delicate fractals,
and a radiant warmth emanates.
In her utter stillness
without thinking, without judgement,
where light is felt, not seen,
when day and night are indistinguishable,
where life and death are one,
she creates and delivers.

She burrows deeper with no exertion,
afloat on the buried river of dreamlessness,
until she surfaces once again,
with a toss of her rumpled hair.
The shadows of leaf buds cast freckles on her shoulders
as she heralds the springtime.

THE WAIT

I hear your cries in the night,
beyond the crickets,
those low moans and long sighs.
There is a graceful bridge,
straight and strong,
that Love created
when it suspended time and space for us.

But I can only wait right now.

You cry for the loss
of what never existed.
You sharpen the blade of each memory
without seeing it truly.
You try to make sense of the senseless
and this can never work.
You want my help with these tasks
when all I desire is to take that cup of poison
from your unsteady hands.

Dear one ...
I will not help you hurt yourself.

But I will rush to your side
when you can at last
sit in the grave carved by your pain.
I will hold your hand and your heart
as sobs turn into anguished howls.
I will lay your head on my lap
as you rest with swollen eyes,
your wounds exposed, raw, and twitching.

Together we will listen
to the pounding of your angry heart,
like the hoof beats of a lone, fenced stallion
on a windy night
or the wings of a moth
bouncing against a burning lantern.

Oh, beloved ...
When will you see what these earthen walls are made of?
Your thoughts have built a prison.
You have been here so long
it feels like home.

Surround Me, Silence

Surround me, my silence
that I may turn my ear
toward the One who speaks
so softly.

Breathing in
I am
drenched
in Love's clarity.

Exhaling,
pouring myself,
I am rain upon a parched riverbed,

I shrink in size
as it all grows lush
and vibrant with life
around me.

And I am a girl once again,
nearly weightless with my joy.

He speaks.
"My little one."

There is a pair of fluttering wings
dancing in my chest.

"Shhhhh… listen."

Love is humming.

LIKE A GHOST

It passes through me like a ghost,
a muffled memory,
leaving the lights on
in chambers bolted long ago,
touching nothing,
taking nothing with it,
leaving another reason for it to return.

One by one I turn the key in rusted locks,
entering the past, counting my steps.
Dimming the lights,
I keep one burning behind me as I go.
Habit or choice? I cannot say.

I feel the shimmer of its lingering essence,
the flash backward in time,
the cool static distance,
containment so intimate
that subatomic particles are still colliding
with settling star dust.

The grip of one breath held too long,
the stutter of a single heartbeat,
the falter in my step,
consciousness stirring,
the quiet haunting,
heat rising.

And like a ghost it is gone.

WITHIN AND WITHOUT

In the clamor of confusion,
she paused,
and breathed
filling her lungs like sails on the open sea,
filled with purest intentions,
welcoming lucent forgiveness,
sensing expansion beyond her form,
until stillness replaced the tumult.

She chose the way of peace.

She watched her thoughts
as if in slow motion.
They became like starling murmurations,
formless and harmless, shifting shape
until one by one each bird drifted away,
swallowed by the sky into nothingness.

Free now, vision clouded no more,
her heart held ripe profusion,
temperate grace
within and without.

And the sweetness of clarity
created rims of light,
golden edges on all she saw.

Love wants nothing.

A PLACE TO REST

To See You

Looking upon you,

I will find the innocent child,

the hero behind the fear,

the victories among the mistakes.

If I listen closely to your words,

and even more so to your silence,

and cherish the trust you offer in this moment,

I will see you.

And I will speak lovingly to you

as I hold your gift of trust against my heart.

No part of you shall I fear.

Nothing shall I judge.

For I have learned to see ...

the Beloved's kiss upon your forehead.

SINGING YOU AWAKE

SINGING YOU AWAKE

In your dreams you are falling,

a swift descent into a dark unknown.

Yet, the bottom never comes.

In your dreams you are flying,

swept away from the trappings of your struggles.

But you know you must return.

In your dreams you are running

from a faceless shadow gaining on you.

So tired but you cannot stop to rest.

In your dreams you are lost.

Time passes, light never dawns.

You wander aimlessly and alone.

Falling, flying, running, lost ...

Darling child, why would I sing you to sleep

when these dreams are waiting?

Beloved, I am singing you awake.

ONENESS

We, though many, are ...

separate in body but one quintessence,

many colors but one prismic field,

many tongues but one harmonic voice,

many ages but one sacred now,

many beliefs but one divine essence,

many suns but one eternal Light,

many lives but one timeless Being.

ABOUT THE AUTHOR AND ARTIST

Dorothy Bury Shaw was born and raised in Chicago, Illinois. She had a very early affinity for art and poetry and a childlike, burgeoning awareness of the rich spiritual plane which would evolve over time. A graduate of the Chicago Academy of Fine Arts, Dorothy initially taught art and freelanced as an editorial illustrator. Her commercial work was primarily published in newspapers and magazines.

Now, focused on her fine art, she is increasingly immersed in the study of myth, tribal legends, sacred texts and folklore. She achieves a rich, other-worldly quality with her images using a painstaking technique, rendering her subjects with intricate layers of ink, watercolor and colored pencil on rag paper. At times she adds collage details. Every line is purposeful, each element is symbolic.

"Where cultures intersect, I find the common ground of our shared human experience, while celebrating all that is spirit within each of us. I am a sacred artist, a seeker and keen observer of the workings of the human heart. As I work, I am softly anchored in ritual repetition as hours pass and my intricate line work emerges. My art is a living prayer, an alchemy of timelessness and mystic truths, a visual chant, an imagery of song."

With her poetry, Dorothy is especially influenced by the Psalmists, the early Persian and Christian mystics, by modern works of several Buddhist monks, by the ancient Hindu scriptures, by prayers and chants in Sanskrit, and by the abundant beautiful verse found in *A Course in Miracles*.

Regarding her poetry, she adds, *"I rest in the arms of the One who formed me as I write my verse, apart from the world, while still in it. I endeavor to see deeply with new eyes and a compassionate heart with those I encounter, and draw from these experiences when I write."*

Dorothy's artwork has won many awards and appeared in distinguished exhibits. It hangs in the homes of collectors in Europe, Israel and across the United States. Her poetry has gained an audience of its own through her art, and this is her first publication. She resides in Downers Grove, Illinois, USA and works from her home studio. Although raised in a Roman Catholic family, and still a practicing Catholic, she respectfully appreciates all spiritual paths. She is married with two daughters, one residing in England. She is an avid reader, enjoys communing with nature, spending time alone in her woodland trailer where she can work on art and write. She relishes one-on-one time with friends and family, caring for and riding her Arab gelding, and enjoying animals of all kinds, both wild and domestic. She is drawn to birds in particular. She is grateful each and every day for her beautifully imperfect life and above all, for the One who dwells within.

To purchase original art or limited edition archival giclée prints
kindly contact the artist through her website at:

www.dburyshaw.com

CPSIA information can be obtained
at www.ICGtesting.com
Printed in the USA
LVHW07n2100100418
573016LV00002B/5/P